SECOND EDITION

TOUCHSTONE

WORKBOOK 3A

MICHAEL MCCARTHY

JEANNE MCCARTEN

HELEN SANDIFORD

CAMBRIDGE
UNIVERSITY PRESS

CAMBRIDGE
UNIVERSITY PRESS

University Printing House, Cambridge CB2 8BS, United Kingdom

One Liberty Plaza, 20th Floor, New York, NY 10006, USA

477 Williamstown Road, Port Melbourne, VIC 3207, Australia

4843/24, 2nd Floor, Ansari Road, Daryaganj, Delhi – 110002, India

79 Anson Road, #06–04/06, Singapore 079906

Cambridge University Press is part of the University of Cambridge.

It furthers the University's mission by disseminating knowledge in the pursuit of education, learning, and research at the highest international levels of excellence.

www.cambridge.org
Information on this title: www.cambridge.org/9781107620827

© Cambridge University Press 2005, 2014

First published 2005
Second Edition 2014

20 19 18 17 16 15 14 13 12 11 10 9 8 7 6 5 4

Printed in the United Kingdom by Latimer Trend

A catalog record for this publication is available from the British Library

ISBN 978-1-107-66583-5 Student's Book
ISBN 978-1-107-62875-5 Student's Book A
ISBN 978-1-107-69446-0 Student's Book B
ISBN 978-1-107-64271-3 Workbook
ISBN 978-1-107-62082-7 Workbook A
ISBN 978-1-107-65147-0 Workbook B
ISBN 978-1-107-62794-9 Full Contact
ISBN 978-1-107-63739-9 Full Contact A
ISBN 978-1-107-63903-4 Full Contact B
ISBN 978-1-107-68094-4 Teacher's Edition with Assessment Audio CD/CD-ROM
ISBN 978-1-107-63179-3 Class Audio CDs (4)

Additional resources for this publication at www.cambridge.org/touchstone2

Contents

1 Opposites

Grammar and vocabulary | **Look at the pictures. Correct the sentences to match the pictures.**

1. Craig is a careful driver.
   Craig is a reckless driver.

2. Lucia always arrives early.
   _____

3. Carlos is waiting impatiently.
   _____

4. Emily walks slowly.
   _____

5. Laila is talking loudly.
   _____

6. Tom seems polite.
   _____

7. Tamara plays tennis badly.
   _____

8. Joe and Kay are dressed informally.
   _____

2 My new job!

Grammar and vocabulary Circle the correct words to complete Cleo's email.

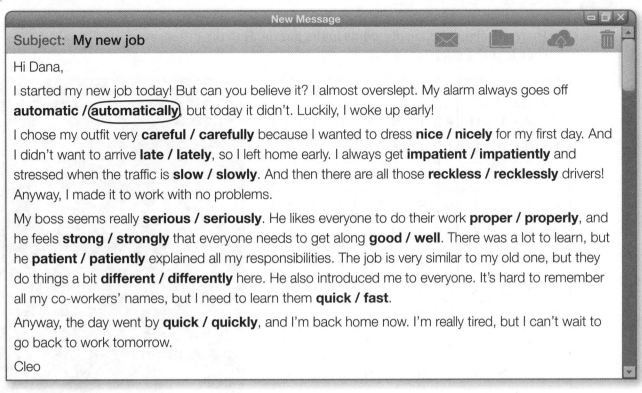

New Message

Subject: **My new job**

Hi Dana,

I started my new job today! But can you believe it? I almost overslept. My alarm always goes off **automatic / ⟨automatically⟩**, but today it didn't. Luckily, I woke up early!

I chose my outfit very **careful / carefully** because I wanted to dress **nice / nicely** for my first day. And I didn't want to arrive **late / lately**, so I left home early. I always get **impatient / impatiently** and stressed when the traffic is **slow / slowly**. And then there are all those **reckless / recklessly** drivers! Anyway, I made it to work with no problems.

My boss seems really **serious / seriously**. He likes everyone to do their work **proper / properly**, and he feels **strong / strongly** that everyone needs to get along **good / well**. There was a lot to learn, but he **patient / patiently** explained all my responsibilities. The job is very similar to my old one, but they do things a bit **different / differently** here. He also introduced me to everyone. It's hard to remember all my co-workers' names, but I need to learn them **quick / fast**.

Anyway, the day went by **quick / quickly**, and I'm back home now. I'm really tired, but I can't wait to go back to work tomorrow.

Cleo

3 Are you fast?

Grammar and vocabulary **A** Complete the answers with an adjective or adverb. Sometimes more than one answer is possible.

1. A Are you a fast reader?

   B No, actually, I read very _____*slowly*_____ .

2. A Do you think you're lazy?

   B No, actually, I'm a _____ worker.

3. A Do you have difficulty remembering names?

   B I don't think so. I remember names very _____ .

4. A Do you eat your meals quickly?

   B Yes, I'm a _____ eater.

5. A Are you a careful driver?

   B Actually, yes. I drive very _____ .

6. A Are you good at sports?

   B Yes, I play most sports _____ .

B Write true answers to the questions in part A.

1. ___*Yes, I am. I read everything very quickly.*___

2. _____

3. _____

4. _____

5. _____

6. _____

1 What are they like?

Vocabulary | **A** There are eight personality words in the puzzle. Find the other seven.
Look in these directions (→↓).

P	R	A	C	T	I	C	A	L	O	D
D	P	L	O	A	T	B	F	K	S	I
L	O	R	E	L	I	A	B	L	E	S
T	G	T	P	E	B	M	D	W	L	O
A	F	V	J	N	P	C	I	H	F	R
Q	B	I	E	T	S	H	V	N	I	G
H	G	E	N	E	R	O	U	S	S	A
R	K	E	L	D	G	O	K	D	H	N
U	O	U	T	G	O	I	N	G	T	I
O	Y	C	R	L	S	Q	E	Y	I	Z
E	A	S	Y	G	O	I	N	G	Q	E
X	B	A	I	H	P	N	T	A	Z	D

B Complete the sentences with the words from part A.

1. My aunt likes to paint. She has creative ideas and is incredibly ___talented___ .

2. My sister is totally _____ . She can never find her car keys and is always losing her cell phone.

3. My friend Steve is extremely down-to-earth and _____ . He gives useful advice.

4. My brother is really _____ . He isn't shy at all.

5. My dad bought me a laptop computer for college. He's very kind and _____ like that.

6. My co-workers are usually good about completing their work. They're fairly _____ .

7. My mom is pretty laid-back and _____ . She never gets upset about anything.

8. My little sister never shares anything. She's so _____ !

2 About you 1

Grammar and vocabulary | Complete each question with the opposite of the adjective given. Then write true answers.

1. Are you honest or ___dishonest___ ? _I'm honest. I always tell the truth._

2. Is your doctor friendly or _____ ? _____

3. Is your best friend reliable or _____ ? _____

4. Are you organized or _____ ? _____

5. Are you patient or _____ ? _____

6. Are your neighbors considerate or _____ ? _____

3 All or nothing

  What's the best next sentence? Circle *a* or *b*.

1. My brother's not talented at all.
   a. He sings, dances, and acts.
   b. He can't sing, dance, or act!

2. My parents are extremely generous.
   a. They give a lot of money to charity.
   b. They give a little money to charity.

3. My sister is incredibly smart.
   a. She's the best student in her class.
   b. She does fairly well in school.

4. My best friend is so funny.
   a. His jokes don't make me laugh at all.
   b. His jokes always make me laugh.

5. My cousin is fairly outgoing.
   a. She never goes to parties.
   b. She sometimes goes to parties.

6. My math teacher is really helpful.
   a. She explains things really well.
   b. She can't explain things clearly.

7. My dad is pretty laid-back.
   a. He gets upset about everything.
   b. He doesn't get upset about most things.

8. My brother is completely inconsiderate.
   a. He never helps around the house.
   b. He sometimes helps me around the house.

4 About you 2

  **Use the expressions in the box to write true sentences about someone you know.
Then add a second sentence about yourself.**

| fairly easygoing | not impatient at all | really practical |
| incredibly friendly | ✓ pretty reliable | very honest |

1. *My older brother's pretty reliable. I think I'm pretty unreliable.*
2. _____
3. _____
4. _____
5. _____
6. _____

1 They're always . . .

Conversation strategies The people in this office don't work very hard. Look at the picture, and write what each person is always doing.

1. Jedd *is always leaving work early* .
2. Reba _____ .
3. John _____ .

4. Kayo _____ .
5. Yasmin _____ .
6. Chad _____ .

2 Individual habits

Conversation strategies Write a response to each statement with *always* and a continuous verb. Use the expressions in the box.

| buy things | ✓ cancel plans | help people | lose stuff | tell jokes |

1. Beth is so unreliable.   I know. *She's always canceling plans!* _____

2. Matt is incredibly disorganized.   That's for sure. _____

3. Elizabeth is very funny.   That's true. _____

4. Theresa isn't practical with money.   You're right. _____

5. Kenny is generous with his time.   Yeah, he is. _____

3 Complaints, complaints

Conversation strategies Complete each conversation with *always* and a continuous verb. Then add *at least* to the response when appropriate. Write *X* if *at least* is not appropriate.

1. **Sam** My sister hardly ever talks to my friends when they come over. She *'s always doing* (do) something else. I mean, she says "Hi," but that's all.

   Fatema Well, _____ she isn't rude to them.

2. **Jody** Last year, my roommate in college _____ (borrow) my books and stuff without asking.

   Pam That's too bad – _____ it sounds like she was really inconsiderate.

3. **Sandy** My last boss was really nice but completely disorganized. She _____ (cancel) meetings at the last minute.

   Natsuko Yeah, _____ it's hard to work for somebody like that.

4. **Daniel** My brother _____ (listen) to music. He's always got his headphones on.

   Sarah Well, _____ his music isn't loud.

5. **Alejandro** I never see my kids these days. They _____ (go) to their friends' houses to play basketball or baseball or something.

   Diana Well, you know, _____ they're interested in sports. A lot of kids just play computer games all the time.

4 About you

Conversation strategies Complete each sentence with true information. Use *always* and a continuous verb.

1. When I was little, *I was always eating candy* _____ .

2. My friends and I _____ .

3. I have some bad habits. I _____ .

4. My best friend _____ .

5. My parents _____ .

6. My favorite teacher in high school _____ .

7. My neighbor _____ .

1 Star qualities

Reading | **A** Read the article. Circle the two adjectives that describe actor Aishwarya Rai in each column.

famous	accomplished	inconsiderate	generous
arrogant	influential	down-to-earth	unfriendly
talented	selfish	beautiful	nice

Aishwarya Rai THE QUEEN OF BOLLYWOOD

Aishwarya Rai is the Queen of Bollywood, India's version of Hollywood and the film capital of the world. With over 18,000 websites devoted to her, she is India's, and possibly the world's, best-known actor.

Aishwarya Rai was born in Mangalore, India, on November 1, 1973. She was raised in a traditional, middle-class family. When she was four, her family moved to Mumbai (Bombay), where she still lives today with her husband, actor Abhishek Bachchan, and their daughter, Aaradhya.

Rai started modeling for fun when she was in college studying architecture. She also received many offers to act. However, her first priority was school, so she said no to all movie offers. Then in 1994, at the age of 21, Rai won the title of Miss World. Soon after that, she accepted her first movie role.

Now an accomplished actor, Rai won Filmfare's Award for Best Actress for her role in *Hum Dil De Chuke Sanam* in 2000. She also starred in Bollywood's most successful international blockbuster, *Devdas*.

Rai acts in five different languages: Hindi, Telugu, Tamil, Bengali, and English.

She is the first Bollywood star to be a juror at the Cannes Film Festival in France, to appear in *Rolling Stone* magazine, and to be on *The Oprah Winfrey Show*. Rai is also the first Indian woman to have a statue in London's wax museum, Madame Tussaud's. In 2012, she received the second highest Order of France.

Aishwarya Rai is one of the most beautiful women in the world, but when Oprah Winfrey asked her about her beauty, she simply said, "Beauty is as beauty does," meaning that what you do is more important than how you look. This is perhaps why Rai created a charitable organization called the Aishwarya Rai Foundation, which helps women, children, the elderly, and animals. She was also named the Goodwill Ambassador for a United Nations program on AIDS in 2012. Her philosophy is very simple: "It's nice to be important, but it's important to be nice."

B Read Rai's biography again. Then correct these false sentences.

with her husband and daughter
1. Aishwarya Rai lives ~~by herself~~ in Mumbai.
2. Rai was born in Mumbai.
3. Rai started modeling in high school.
4. Rai studied acting in college.
5. Rai won the title of Miss World when she was 19.
6. Rai makes movies in four languages.
7. Rai has a statue in Cannes, France.
8. Rai feels that it's important to be beautiful.

2 She's admirable.

A Use the words and expressions in the box to complete the profile of Midori Goto.

accomplished	called	started
at the age of	can be	✓ was born and raised

Midori Goto

Midori Goto is an incredibly talented violinist. She _was born and raised_ in Osaka, Japan. She _____ studying the violin with her mother, and _____ seven, she gave her first public performance in Osaka.

Studying music _____ very demanding, as well as rewarding. When she was only 10, Midori moved to New York City to study music at the Juilliard School. She also attended the Professional Children's School for her academic studies. By the time Midori turned 11, she was already an _____ artist and had performed with the New York Philharmonic.

Midori is also very generous. In 1992, she created an organization _____ Midori & Friends that provides free music education for children in city schools.

Midori is now a professor of music at the University of Southern California.

B Write a short profile about someone you admire.

Unit 1 Progress chart

What can you do? Mark the boxes. ✓ = I can . . . ？ = I need to review how to . . .	To review, go back to these pages in the Student's Book.
Grammar	
☐ use manner adverbs and adjectives correctly.	2 and 3
☐ use regular and irregular adverbs.	3
☐ use adverbs to make adjectives and adverbs stronger.	5
☐ add prefixes to adjectives to make opposites.	5
Vocabulary	
☐ name at least 12 adverbs.	2, 3, 4, and 5
☐ name at least 15 personality adjectives.	4 and 5
Conversation strategies	
☐ use *always* and a continuous verb to describe individual habits.	6
☐ use *at least* to point out the positive side of a situation.	7
Writing	
☐ write a short profile about someone.	9

Experiences

Lesson A / Hopes and dreams

1 Have you or haven't you?

Grammar **A** Read the "to do" list. What things have you done? What things haven't you done? Write true sentences using the present perfect.

Things I want to do

1. drive a sports car
2. go skiing
3. learn a second language
4. see the Taj Mahal
5. study photography
6. travel to Europe
7. try windsurfing
8. surf in Hawai'i

1. _I haven't driven a sports car._   5. _____
2. _____   6. _____
3. _____   7. _____
4. _____   8. _____

B Complete the sentences using the present perfect and the expressions in the "to do" list in part A. Use the negative form where necessary.

1. My cousin _has driven a sports car_____ once or twice. He loves to drive.

2. My sister and I _____ many times. We love the snow.

3. Each of my brothers _____ . One speaks Mandarin and one speaks Cantonese.

4. We _____ , but I really want to go to India one day.

5. My teacher _____ . She takes beautiful travel photos.

6. My parents _____ before, but they hope to go next year.

7. My older brother _____ . He's afraid of the water.

8. My best friend _____ , but she wants to go this summer.

2 I've tried . . .

Grammar | **Write sentences with the present perfect.**

1. My teacher (go / many times) to the United States.
   My teacher's been to the United States many times.
   or *My teacher's gone to the United States many times.*

2. My boss (ski / several times) in the Swiss Alps.
   _____

3. I (always / want) to go on a roller coaster.
   _____

4. My neighbor (never / go / before) to Canada.
   _____

5. My parents (see / five times) the movie *Titanic*.
   _____

6. My brothers (try / once or twice) Vietnamese food.
   _____

7. My best friend (never / see) the ocean.
   _____

8. I (never / have) the money to take a vacation.
   _____

3 About you

Grammar | **Answer the questions with true information. Add a frequency expression where necessary.**

1. What's something exciting you've done?
   I've gone hang gliding once.

2. What's something scary you've done?
   _____

3. What's something boring you've done in the last month?
   _____

4. How many times have you been late to class recently?
   _____

5. What country have you always wanted to visit?
   _____

6. What kind of food have you never tried before?
   _____

7. What movie have you seen several times?
   _____

8. What's something you've never done, but always wanted to do?
   _____

1 Have you ever . . . ?

Grammar | **Complete the conversations with the simple past or present perfect.**

1. A __*Have*__ you ever __*gone*__ (go) cliff diving?

   B No, I _____ . It sounds too scary!
   _____ you _____ (do) it?

   A Yeah, I _____ (go) last weekend.

   B Wow! You're brave. How _____ (be) it?

   A It was incredible! I _____ (love) it.

2. A I _____ never _____ (travel) alone.
   How about you?

   B No, but I _____ always _____ (want) to. I'm
   sure it's exciting.

   A I think so, too. Do you know my friend Jill?
   She _____ (take) a hiking trip alone last year.

   B I know. I _____ (speak) to her about it last week.

3. A _____ you ever _____ (try) horseback riding?

   B Yeah. I actually _____ (do) it once several years
   ago.

   A Really? _____ you _____ (like) it?

   B No, not really. It _____ (be) very scary.

   A Oh, too bad. I go all the time. I _____ (get) really
   good at it.

4. A _____ you _____ (do) anything special
   last weekend?

   B Yes. My family and I _____ (take) a ride in a hot-air
   balloon! _____ you ever _____ (be) up
   in one?

   A No, I _____ . _____ you _____ (enjoy) it?

   B Yeah, we _____ (love) every minute! It was amazing!

2 Yes or no?

Grammar
and
vocabulary

Complete the questions with the simple past or present perfect form of the verbs in the box. Then answer the questions with true information.

| break   eat   ✓go   have   lose   ride   visit   win |

1. ___Did___ you ___go___ to the zoo yesterday? _No, I didn't go to the zoo yesterday._
2. _____ you ever _____ your leg? _____
3. _____ you ever _____ a spelling contest? _____
4. _____ you _____ a bike to class yesterday? _____
5. _____ you _____ your grandparents last summer? _____
6. _____ you ever _____ a bad cold? _____
7. _____ you _____ a big breakfast this morning? _____
8. _____ you ever _____ your wallet? _____

3 About you

Grammar

Use the cues to write questions in the simple past or present perfect. Then write true answers.

1. (try any new foods on your last vacation)
   Did you try any new foods on your last vacation?
   Yes, I did. I tried oysters. They're delicious.

2. (ever / hike in the mountains)
   _____
   _____

3. (see a lot of movies last summer)
   _____
   _____

4. (ever / walk across a tightrope)
   _____
   _____

5. (ever / find a lost wallet or cell phone)
   _____
   _____

6. (ever / forget an important appointment)
   _____
   _____

1 Tell me more!

Conversation strategies | **Complete the conversations with the responses in the box.**

Cool. Do you have a favorite place?   That sounds great. How do you get there?
I've heard her tests are hard. How did you do?   That's too bad. Did you study for it?
Oh, that sounds hard. Did you finish?   ✓ Yeah, I am. Do you want to come?

1. **Jake** Hey, Alex! Are you going surfing this weekend?

     Alex *Yeah, I am. Do you want to come?*

     Jake Well, I'm working this weekend. And, actually, I've never surfed before.

     Alex Really? I started surfing three years ago, and now I can't stop.

     Jake _____

     Alex Yeah, I like to go to Cove Beach. Have you heard of it?

     Jake Yeah, I have, but I've never been there.

     Alex You should come sometime. I can teach you the basics.

     Jake _____

     Alex I usually drive. You can ride your bike there, but it's a little far.

     Jake All right. Tell me the next time you're planning to go.

2. **Ki-Won** Hi, Erin. You look upset. What's wrong?

     Erin I just took Mrs. Chen's English test.

     Ki-Won _____

     Erin I don't think I did too well.

     Ki-Won _____

     Erin Yeah, I studied really hard.

     Ki-Won Was it an essay or a multiple-choice test?

     Erin Well, it was both. There were 30 multiple-choice questions *and* an essay question!

     Ki-Won _____

     Erin Yeah, I finished it, but I didn't have time to check my answers.

     Ki-Won Well, maybe you did better than you think!

2 Did you?

Conversation strategies Complete each conversation with a response question to show interest.

1. A I went on an amazing roller coaster last weekend.

    B *Did you?*____ That sounds like fun.

2. A I love going to the movies!

    B _____ Let's go sometime!

3. A I won first prize in the art contest!

    B _____ That's wonderful!

4. A I'm scared of snakes and spiders.

    B _____ I am too.

5. A I ride my motorcycle on the weekends.

    B _____ I've never ridden a motorcycle.

6. A I've broken my arm twice.

    B _____ That's too bad.

7. A It's my birthday today. I'm 18!

    B _____ Happy birthday!

8. A I've seen that documentary about fast food four times.

    B _____ What's it about exactly?

3 Extreme sports

Conversation strategies Respond to these statements with a response question. Then add a follow-up question to ask for more information.

1. In the summer, I love to go hang gliding. *Do you? Is it scary?*_____

2. I've gone scuba diving several times. _____

3. Last spring, I went deep-sea fishing. _____

4. I'm a pretty good windsurfer. _____

5. I absolutely love sailing. _____

6. I started surfing last year. _____

1 Finally here!

Reading | **A** Read Gisele's travel blog about her trip to China. What is one thing she has always wanted to do?

Gisele's Blog

Finally here!

We arrived in Chengdu, the capital of Sichuan province, the day before yesterday. Exhausted, we went straight to bed, but got up early yesterday. We took a bus to Mount Emei. Fortunately, it's close to Chengdu, so we had a full day to explore. Mount Emei is beautiful, and it has lots of temples and monasteries.

Today we went to Leshan to see the giant Buddha statue. It's the largest stone Buddha in the world and was cut into a cliff. It took 90 years to make. It's huge—233 feet (71 meters) high!

Our hotel in Chengdu is inexpensive and very nice. We met some people from Canada last night. We all went out for some delicious Sichuan food.

We're going to the Giant Panda Nature Reserve tomorrow. I've always wanted to see a baby panda. I'm so excited. Have any of you been there? What's the best way to get there?

Posted January 25 at 7:57 p.m.

JOE TRIP Re: Finally here!

I went to see the pandas last year. It was pretty cool. You're going to love it. There are regular buses from Chengdu, and the bus ride usually takes three hours. But go early to see the pandas when they're awake.

Posted January 25 at 9 p.m.

Last day in Chengdu

We went to the Panda Reserve yesterday. I was able to see some baby pandas. They are so cute. They do amazing things at the Reserve to save these animals.

Posted January 27 at 10 a.m.

Wow!

We just spent a few days in western Sichuan. It was really interesting. Tonight we head to Beijing. I really want to see the Forbidden City, Tiananmen Square, and the Bird's Nest Stadium. This really is a fantastic trip.

Posted February 2 at 4:45 p.m.

B Read the blog again. Then answer the questions.

1. When did Gisele arrive in Chengdu? *She arrived in Chengdu on January 23.*

2. What did she see first? _____

3. Who did she meet at the hotel? _____

4. When does Joe Trip think Gisele should go to see the pandas? _____

5. Where did Gisele go after Chengdu? _____

6. Where is Gisele going tonight? _____

2 Fortunately, . . .

Writing **A** Read Ian's blog entry about his trip to Belize. Complete the sentences with *fortunately*, *unfortunately*, or *amazingly*. Sometimes more than one answer is possible.

Ian's Blog

We were very tired when we got off the plane in Belize City, but ___*fortunately*___ , our host was there to meet us. _____ , the airline lost my luggage, so I left the airport without it. We got on a bus and headed for Maya Mountain Lodge. _____ , when we got to the lodge, the airline called to say my luggage was on its way. The next morning, we set out on our first day trip. The mountain road was narrow and winding. _____ , we had a careful driver. Our first stop was at a big waterfall. _____ , it was raining when we got there, so we just took pictures from the bus. Our next stop was at a river called Rio on Pools. By then it was sunny, so everyone went swimming. _____ , I didn't have my bathing suit with me, so I couldn't swim. The views were beautiful, and I took a lot of photos. I'm not usually a very good photographer, but _____ , my pictures turned out really well.

B Write a blog entry about one of the following experiences. Use adverbs like *fortunately* and *amazingly* to show your feelings about what happened.

- Competing in a contest
- Having a fun picnic
- Taking an exciting trip
- Trying a new activity

Blog

Unit 2 Progress chart

What can you do? Mark the boxes. ✔ = I can . . . ? = I need to review how to . . .	To review, go back to these pages in the Student's Book.
Grammar ☐ use the present perfect with regular and irregular verbs.	12 and 13
☐ use the present perfect to say what I have and haven't done.	13, 14, and 15
☐ ask and answer questions beginning with *Have you ever . . . ?*	14 and 15
☐ use the simple past to answer questions in the present perfect.	14 and 15
Vocabulary ☐ name at least 12 irregular past participles.	13, 14, and 15
Conversation strategies ☐ keep a conversation going by showing interest.	16
☐ use *Do you?*, *Did you?*, *Are you?*, or *Have you?* to show interest.	17
Writing ☐ use adverbs to show my feelings about something.	19

Wonders of the world

Lesson A | Human wonders

1 That's expensive!

Grammar and vocabulary | Complete the questions with superlatives. Then match the questions with the correct pictures and information below.

1. What's _the most expensive_ (expensive) musical instrument ever sold? _h_
2. Which country has _____ (long) school year? _____
3. What sport has _____ (fans) in the world? _____
4. Who was _____ (young) number-one classical artist? _____
5. Where's _____ (narrow) house in the world? _____
6. What's _____ (famous) statue in the United States? _____
7. What's one of _____ (tall) hotels in the world? _____
8. What's _____ (fast) car in the world? _____

a

The Burj al-Arab Hotel in Dubai is 321 meters (1,060 feet) tall.

b

Almost 4 million people visit the Statue of Liberty each year.

c

Millions of fans around the world watch soccer.

d

The Thrust SSC went up to 1,227 kilometers (763 miles) per hour.

e

Welsh soprano Charlotte Church was only 12 years old when her album, *Voice of an Angel*, sold over 2 million copies in the UK.

f

Chinese children go to school 251 days a year.

g

The Keret House in Warsaw, Poland, is less than 1.5 meters (5 feet) at its widest point.

h

"The Lady Tennant" violin by Antonio Stradivari sold at auction for over $2 million.

2 It's the best.

Grammar | **Complete the conversations. Use superlative adjectives.**

1. A That's a really big airplane.

   B Yeah. It's _the biggest_ airplane I've ever seen.

2. A It's really easy to get to the airport by subway.

   B Right. It's definitely _____ way to get there.

3. A This restaurant isn't expensive at all.

   B I know. It's _____ place to eat around here.

4. A This subway is really crowded.

   B Yeah, it is. Actually, it's always _____ subway line.

5. A Look at that cruise ship. It's so big!

   B It's the *Oasis of the Seas*. It's one of _____ cruise ships in the world.

6. A Wow. I like your watch. It's so thin.

   B I know. It's _____ watch I've ever seen.

7. A This is a pretty good price for these pants.

   B Yes, it is. Actually, I think this store has _____ prices in the mall.

8. A This is a nice gallery, but the new exhibition has some really bad paintings.

   B Yeah. They're some of _____ paintings I've ever seen.

3 About you

Grammar | **Complete the questions with superlatives. Then write true answers.**

1. Where's _the cheapest_ (cheap) place to go shopping around here?

   The cheapest place to go shopping is downtown.

2. And where's _____ (bad) place to go shopping?

   _____

3. Which neighborhood has _____ (many) restaurants?

   _____

4. What's _____ (quiet) neighborhood in your city?

   _____

5. What's _____ (amazing) building you've ever seen?

   _____

6. Which neighborhood has _____ (a lot of) traffic?

   _____

7. What's _____ (wonderful) city you've ever visited?

   _____

8. Where can you buy _____ (delicious) pastries in your city?

   _____

1 Wonders of the earth

Vocabulary | **A** Look at the pictures and complete the puzzle. Then write the answer to the question below.

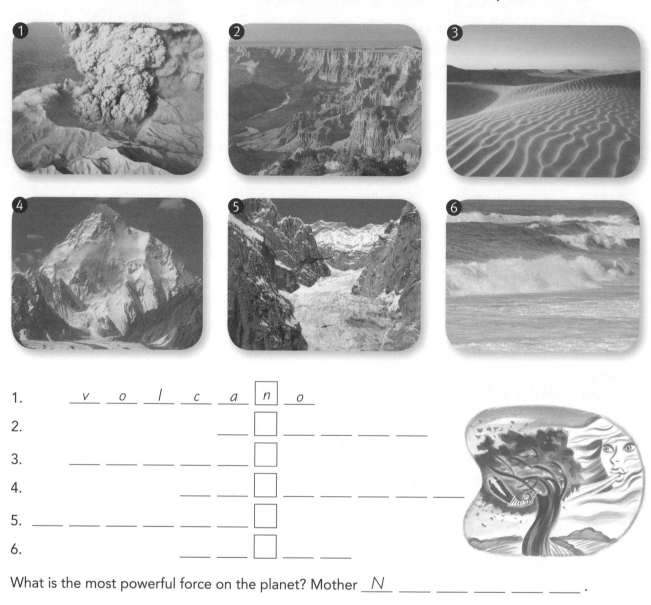

1.   _v_ _o_ _l_ _c_ _a_ [n] _o_
2.   ___ ___ [ ] ___ ___ ___ ___ ___
3.   ___ ___ ___ [ ] ___ ___
4.   ___ ___ ___ [ ] ___ ___ ___ ___
5.   ___ ___ ___ ___ [ ] ___ ___ ___
6.   ___ ___ [ ] ___ ___ ___

What is the most powerful force on the planet? Mother _N_ ___ ___ ___ ___ ___ .

B Complete these sentences with the words from part A.

1. The Grand _Canyon_ in Arizona is 1,600 meters (5,249 feet) deep in some parts.

2. The Pacific _____ is about ten times larger than the Arctic.

3. K2, the second highest _____ in the world, is 8,610 meters (28,250 feet) high.

4. In the Sahara _____ , temperatures can reach 54 degrees Celsius (130 degrees Fahrenheit).

5. The Siachen, with more than 57 billion cubic meters of ice, is one of the world's largest _____ .

6. Mt. Pinatubo in the Philippines is an active _____ . It last erupted in 1991.

2 How wide?

Grammar | **Look at the pictures. Complete each question with *How* + adjective. Then write the answers.**

1. Q <u>*How wide*</u> are the Khone Falls on the Mekong River?
   A <u>*They're 10.8 kilometers wide.*</u>

2. Q _____ is the Amazon Rain Forest?
   A _____

3. Q _____ can it get in Antarctica?
   A _____

4. Q _____ is the Mississippi River?
   A _____

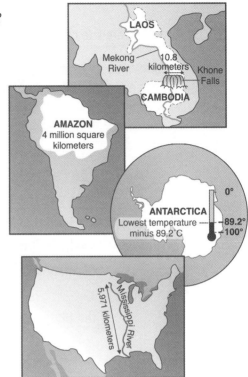

3 Discover New Zealand!

Grammar | **Write *How* questions based on the guidebook page. Then answer the questions.**

1. Q <u>*How big is the North Island?*</u>
   A <u>*It's 115,777 square kilometers.*</u>

2. Q _____
   A _____

3. Q _____
   A _____

4. Q _____
   A _____

5. Q _____
   A _____

6. Q _____
   A _____

7. Q _____
   A _____

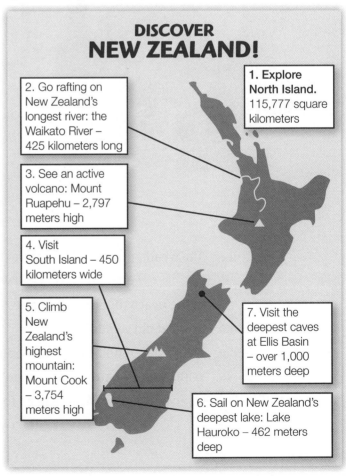

DISCOVER NEW ZEALAND!

1. Explore North Island. 115,777 square kilometers

2. Go rafting on New Zealand's longest river: the Waikato River – 425 kilometers long

3. See an active volcano: Mount Ruapehu – 2,797 meters high

4. Visit South Island – 450 kilometers wide

5. Climb New Zealand's highest mountain: Mount Cook – 3,754 meters high

6. Sail on New Zealand's deepest lake: Lake Hauroko – 462 meters deep

7. Visit the deepest caves at Ellis Basin – over 1,000 meters deep

1 Really?

Conversation strategies **A** Complete the conversations with the sentences in the box.

It really was.	It sure is.	They really are.	✓Yeah, it really is.
It sure does.	Really? I didn't know that.	We really should.	

1. **Danielle** I think Hawai'i is one of the most interesting states in the U.S.

   Mark _Yeah, it really is._ _____ You know, more than one-third of the world's pineapples are from Hawai'i.

   Danielle Really? I didn't know that. I know it has some of the best surfing in the world, though.

   Mark _____ They get some of the highest waves there. And did you know all eight islands are volcanoes? . . .

2. **Mee** Mount Sorak in South Korea is so beautiful, especially in the fall.

   Kyong _____ I love it there. Have you ever gone hiking there?

   Mee Uh-huh, I've hiked there several times with my friends.

   Kyong _____

   Mee Yeah. The waterfalls are the best.

   Kyong Yeah. _____

3. **Chika** The weather was terrible last weekend.

   Kacie _____ I wanted to go to the beach, but it was too cold.

   Chika So what did you do?

   Kacie Well, I stayed home and watched movies.

   Chika Yeah? Well, I heard next weekend's going to be warm and sunny. We should go to the beach then.

   Kacie _____ Let's plan on going then.

2 The best and the worst!

Conversation strategies | Complete the conversations with superlative adjectives for emphasis.

1. A Chichén Itzá in Mexico has _the coolest_ (cool) Mayan ruins. Have you ever been there?

   B Yeah, I had _____ (good) time at the pyramids.

2. A The food at that restaurant was _____ (bad)!

   B I know, but at least the waiter was nice.

3. A How was your weekend?

   B Wonderful! We went to _____ (incredible) lake and rented a boat. We just sailed around for hours!

4. A Have you ever hiked the Appalachian Trail?

   B No, I haven't. But I hear it has _____ (amazing) scenery.

3 It really is the best!

Conversation strategies | You're camping with your friend. Write responses with *really* or *sure* to show you are a supportive listener. Then add a sentence using a superlative adjective for emphasis.

1. It feels really good to be on vacation.   *It sure does! And camping was the coolest idea!*

2. Our hike yesterday was great. _____

3. We should go swimming in the lake today. _____

4. It's so nice to be in the country. _____

4 About you

Conversation strategies | Write true sentences about your last vacation or trip. Use superlative adjectives for emphasis.

1. I went _to Costa Rica last year. They have the most amazing beaches_ .
2. I stayed _____ .
3. I saw _____ .
4. I met _____ .
5. I ate _____ .
6. I visited _____ .

1 The coldest continent

Reading **A** Look at the topics below. Then read the article and write the number of the paragraph where the topic is explained in detail.

_3_ the driest weather   ____ the strongest winds

____ the most time zones   ____ the most ice

____ the smallest population   ____ the most daylight

____ the farthest south   ____ the coldest temperature

AMAZING ANTARCTICA

Vostok Station

1 Antarctica is the coldest, windiest, and driest continent on Earth. It's the fifth largest of the world's seven continents. A layer of ice almost 5 kilometers (3 miles) thick covers the island in some places. In fact, 90% of the world's ice is in Antarctica.

2 The weather in Antarctica is the coldest on Earth. The lowest temperature ever recorded, –89.2 degrees Celsius (–128.6 degrees Fahrenheit), was in 1983 at the Vostok Station, an old Russian research base. At the South Pole, the temperature varies from –35 degrees Celsius (–31 degrees Fahrenheit) in the midsummer to –70 degrees Celsius (–94 degrees Fahrenheit) in the midwinter.

3 Antarctica is not only the world's coldest continent but also the driest place on Earth. Sometimes called the world's largest desert, it gets about the same amount of rain each year as the Sahara. Antarctic winds are the strongest on the planet, reaching up to 320 kilometers (199 miles) per hour.

4 Located at the South Pole, Antarctica is the farthest south of any continent. The South Pole gets six months of nonstop daylight from September through March. Then it gets six months of nonstop darkness. And because it's so far south, Antarctica covers the most time zones – all of them!

5 Explorers first visited Antarctica in 1821. Then in 1899, a Norwegian explorer set up a research station on Antarctica, and for the first time, people could live there. Now there are about 60 research bases there, set up by many different countries. The population of Antarctica grows from about 1,000 in the winter to about 4,000 during the summer. It has the smallest population of any continent.

B Read the article again. Write *T* (true) or *F* (false) for each sentence. Then correct the false sentences.

1. Antarctica is the world's ~~seventh~~ largest continent. _F_
   fifth

2. Antarctica has 90% of the world's ice. ____

3. Antarctica gets more rain than the Sahara Desert. ____

4. Antarctica's six months of nonstop daylight begins in March. ____

5. About 1,000 people live in Antarctica during the summer. ____

2 The dry facts

Writing **A** Read the facts about the Sahara. Combine each pair of sentences to form one sentence.

1	**2**	**3**	**4**
The Sahara is the largest hot desert in the world. It covers 9.1 million square kilometers of land in North Africa.	The sand dunes are the highest dunes in the world. They are the biggest tourist attraction in the Sahara.	The Qattara Depression in Egypt's Sahara is one of the lowest points in Africa. It is 133 meters below sea level.	The Libyan Sahara is the driest place in the desert. It has the least amount of animal or plant life.

1. _The Sahara, the largest hot desert in the world, covers 9.1 million square kilometers of land in North Africa._

2. _____

3. _____

4. _____

B Write four to six pieces of information about your favorite place. Then combine the facts to make sentences.

Unit 3 Progress chart

What can you do? Mark the boxes. ☑ = I can . . . ? = I need to review how to . . .	To review, go back to these pages in the Student's Book.
☐ use the superlative form of adjectives. ☐ use the superlative with nouns. ☐ ask and answer questions using *how* + adjective.	22 and 23 22 and 23 24 and 25
☐ name 5 human wonders. ☐ name 5 natural wonders.	21, 22, and 23 21, 24, and 25
☐ use short responses with *really* and *sure* to show I'm a supportive listener. ☐ use superlative adjectives to emphasize my opinions or feelings.	26 27
☐ add information about a place or thing in sentences.	29

Grammar

Vocabulary

Conversation strategies

Writing

25

Family life

1 Family obligations

Grammar | **Complete the conversations with the correct form of the verbs in the box.**

change	do	help	read	think
clean	do	play	stay	✓watch

1. Jeff   When I was young, my parents never let me ___watch___ TV.
    Paul   Really? Why not?
    Jeff   They wanted me _____ books and _____ about
            the stories, not just watch TV.
    Paul   My parents were pretty easygoing about watching TV.
    Jeff   What do you mean?
    Paul   Well, they just made me _____ my homework first.
            Then I could watch all the TV I wanted.

2. Liz   I heard you broke your arm. What happened?
    Kaya   My grandmother asked me _____ a lightbulb
           in the ceiling fan. I lost my balance and fell off
           a ladder.
    Liz   Ouch! What did your doctor say?
    Kaya   He told me _____ home for a week.
    Liz   Yeah. And you should get someone _____
           you next time.

3. Kyle   I hate Mondays!
    Naomi   Me too. They're the worst.
    Kyle   Yeah, Monday is when my mom has
             me _____ the entire house.
    Naomi   Really? By yourself? My brother always
             helps me _____ my chores.
    Kyle   Well, my little sister never helps.
             My mom just lets her _____
             video games all day!
    Naomi   That's not fair!

2 Gripes and grumbles

Grammar and vocabulary | Complete the sentences using the words given.

1. My brother loves anchovies.
   He can't _get me to try one_ .
   (get / try one)

2. My father is pretty strict.
   He always _____ .
   (have / come home early)

3. My parents want me to be a pianist.
   They _____ .
   (make / practice every day)

4. My sister is always watching TV.
   She never _____ .
   (let / have the remote)

5. My daughter is always on her cell phone.
   She always _____ .
   (want / pay the bill)

6. My parents never have enough time to cook.
   They often _____ .
   (ask / prepare dinner)

7. My kids don't like to clean.
   They rarely _____ .
   (help / wash the dishes)

8. My grandfather can't hear very well.
   He always _____ .
   (tell / speak louder)

3 About you

Grammar | Complete these sentences with true information.

1. My parents want me _to go to a really competitive college_ .
2. My best friend often asks me _____ .
3. Our English teacher sometimes has us _____ .
4. I always tell my friend _____ .
5. I can't get my family members _____ .
6. Parents shouldn't let their kids _____ .
7. My friends sometimes help me _____ .
8. I can't make my parents _____ .
9. My mom always has me _____ .
10. I'm always telling my friend _____ .

1 My family tree

Vocabulary | **Look at Kelly's family tree. Then complete the sentences with the words in the box.**

aunt	brother-in-law	great-grandmother	✓immediate	niece	stepmother
blended	cousin	half brothers	nephew	stepdaughter	uncle

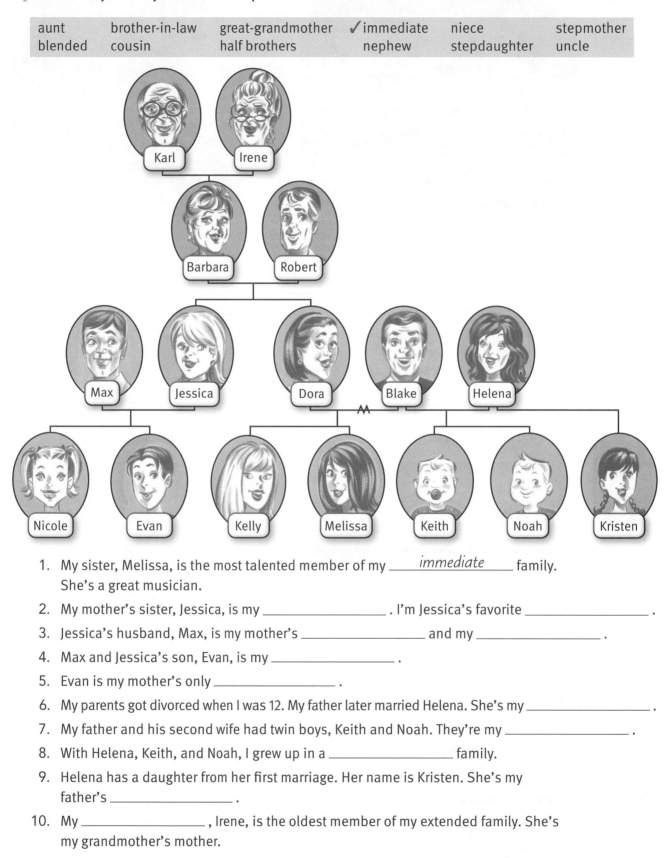

1. My sister, Melissa, is the most talented member of my ___immediate___ family. She's a great musician.

2. My mother's sister, Jessica, is my _____ . I'm Jessica's favorite _____ .

3. Jessica's husband, Max, is my mother's _____ and my _____ .

4. Max and Jessica's son, Evan, is my _____ .

5. Evan is my mother's only _____ .

6. My parents got divorced when I was 12. My father later married Helena. She's my _____ .

7. My father and his second wife had twin boys, Keith and Noah. They're my _____ .

8. With Helena, Keith, and Noah, I grew up in a _____ family.

9. Helena has a daughter from her first marriage. Her name is Kristen. She's my father's _____ .

10. My _____ , Irene, is the oldest member of my extended family. She's my grandmother's mother.

2 When I was a kid, . . .

Grammar and vocabulary | Complete the conversation with *used to* or *would* and the verbs given. Sometimes more than one answer is possible.

Tia Hi, Mom. What are you looking at?

Mom I'm looking at some old pictures from when I was a kid.

Tia Cool. Who's this boy?

Mom That's my friend Jay. He _used to live_ next door to me.
(live)

We _'d spend / used to spend_ every day together in the summer.
(spend)

Tia Really? Doing what?

Mom We _____ to ride bikes.
(love)

We _____ our lunches and spend the whole day riding in the woods.
(bring)

Tia Cool. What else?

Mom Well, we _____ fishing, and my mom _____ whatever
(go)   (always cook)

fish we caught.

Tia It sounds like you had a lot of fun.

Mom We did. We _____ an old black-and-white TV, and we _____
(have)   (watch)

horror movies all the time.

Tia Black-and-white TV? You mean you didn't have a color TV?

Mom No, we didn't. And we didn't have remotes, either.

Tia Wow. I can't even imagine!

3 About you

Grammar | Are these sentences true or false for you? Write *T* (true) or *F* (false). Then correct the false sentences.

1. _F_ When I was a kid, I used to go to the movies on Saturdays.
    I didn't use to go to the movies on Saturdays. I would play with my brother.

2. ____ Our neighbors used to have a pet rabbit.
    _____

3. ____ I used to hate pizza.
    _____

4. ____ My parents used to make me go to bed before 9:00.
    _____

5. ____ I used to ride my bike to school every day.
    _____

6. ____ My family used to live in a small house in the country.
    _____

1 What's your opinion?

Read the news items. Then write your opinions using the expressions in the box.

I don't think	If you ask me,	It seems to me (that)
I think	It seems like	

> The percentage of obese children and adolescents has tripled in the last 30 years.

1. _If you ask me, children and adolescents don't exercise enough these days._

> Learning a language after age 14 is not required in British schools.

2. _____

> Surveys show South Korean teens get a new cell phone every year.

3. _____

> Most Japanese high schools don't allow their students to hold part-time jobs.

4. _____

> Russia has one of the world's highest divorce rates.

5. _____

> North American children are spending more time on their computers than they do outside.

6. _____

2 I agree.

Follow the instructions and complete the conversations. Use the expressions in the box.

Absolutely.	✓ I agree with you.	That's true.
Definitely.	Oh, I know.	You're right.

1. Bruno   I think there's a lot of pressure on young couples these days.

   You   _I agree with you._
   (Tell Bruno you agree.)

   Bruno   They work longer hours and still don't make much money.

   You   _____
   (Tell Bruno you're in definite agreement.)

2. Salma   If you ask me, our teachers give us too much homework.

   You   _____ I never have any time to spend with my family.
   (Tell Salma you're in absolute agreement.)

   Salma   And we never get a break. We even get homework over school vacations.

   You   _____
   (Tell Salma she's right.)

3. Ciara   It seems like a lot of elderly people live alone.

   You   _____
   (Tell Ciara her information is true.)

   Ciara   It's terrible when families don't spend time with their elderly relatives.

   You   _____
   (Tell Ciara you know.)

3 Don't you agree?

Your friend is telling you his or her opinion. Agree and give an appropriate response.

1. I think even little kids need cell phones these days.

   Definitely. I think they're good in an emergency.

2. If you ask me, movie tickets cost too much.

   _____

3. It seems to me that people eat too much fast food.

   _____

4. I think everyone should learn a second language.

   _____

5. I don't think people take enough vacation time.

   _____

1 Gripes from a stay-at-home dad

Reading | **A** Read the posts on a social network. What kind of thread is it?

☐ academic   ☐ news   ☐ personal   ☐ travel

Mark's Page

Mark Santos

What a day! I'm exhausted. I had to nag the kids to get them to help me around the house and clean up because their five cousins are coming for dinner. My brother and sister-in-law are going out for their anniversary. Can you imagine – eight kids for dinner? Also, my aunt wants to come over to see all her great-nieces and -nephews. To top it all off, my wife, Laura, is away on a business trip, so I have to do all the cooking myself. Any ideas for what to make?

One hour ago

Mei-ling Lee   Why don't you ask Laura? She's the best cook! Can you get in touch with her?

One hour ago

Mark Santos   Right, Mei-ling. Well, right now she's on a flight to Beijing. Before she got this new job, we used to make dinner together most nights. Now that she's working longer hours and traveling more, I guess it's more up to me.

45 minutes ago

Ann Wilkerson   Here's an idea: when our kids were younger, we used to make tacos. The kids can help you get everything ready, and then they can make their own. You just need to get everyone to help.

30 minutes ago

Mark Santos   Thanks, Ann. That's a great idea. I'll call my brother and have him do some shopping on the way here. I'll get the hang of being a stay-at-home dad pretty soon. Laura's happy traveling, and I'm more of a homebody, so I think it'll work out.

20 minutes ago

B Look at the words and expressions. Find them in the posts, and choose the correct meaning.

1. nag _b_   a. talk loudly   b. ask a lot of times   c. laugh quietly

2. great-niece _____   a. your favorite niece   b. your niece's mother   c. your niece's daughter

3. to top it all off _____   a. the last problem is   b. fortunately   c. one good thing is

4. get the hang of _____   a. stop   b. understand   c. dislike

5. homebody _____   a. someone who doesn't   b. a housekeeper   c. a personal chef
                           like to go out

C Read the posts again. Then answer the questions.

1. How many children does Mark have?

2. How many kids are coming for dinner?

3. Why is his aunt coming over?

4. Who used to do the cooking?

5. What is Mark going to make?

2 Lessons learned

A Read the journal entry. Then complete the sentences with the expressions in the box.

In those days	Nowadays	Today	When I was a kid

March 8

I just bought some lemonade from some kids on the corner near my apartment. It brought back so many memories! _____ , I used to make lemonade with my brother. We'd set up a stand in front of our house and sell the lemonade to people walking down the street. _____ , we didn't worry about money, and we drank more lemonade than we sold. _____ , I still remember the lesson that experience taught me — don't drink your profits! I don't think we ever made any money, but it sure was a lot of fun. _____ we have air conditioning, but I still like a cold cup of lemonade on a hot day.

B Write a journal entry about a childhood memory you remember clearly. Use the expressions from part A.

_____

_____

_____

_____

_____

_____

_____

_____

Unit 4 Progress chart

What can you do? Mark the boxes. ☑ = I can . . .　　？ = I need to review how to . . .	To review, go back to these pages in the Student's Book.
Grammar　☐ use *let*, *make*, *have*, *get*, *want*, *ask*, *tell*, and *help*.	34 and 35
☐ use *used to* and *would* to talk about memories.	36 and 37
Vocabulary　☐ name at least 15 family members.	36
Conversation strategies　☐ give opinions with expressions like *I think* and *It seems to me*.	38
☐ use expressions like *absolutely*, *exactly*, and *you're right* to agree.	39
Writing　☐ use time markers to write about the past and the present.	41

33

A bag and a can

Vocabulary | Look at the pictures. Complete the sentences with the expressions in the box.
Some expressions are used more than once.

a bag of	a box of	a carton of	a package of
a bottle of	a can of	a jar of	

1. In the United States, you can buy
    a bottle of milk or _____ milk.

2. In Thailand, you can buy _____
    curry paste or _____ curry paste.

3. In Japan, you can buy _____
    crackers or _____ crackers.

4. In Australia, you can buy _____
    asparagus or _____ asparagus.

5. In Colombia, you can buy _____
    coffee or _____ coffee.

6. In France, you can buy _____
    soup or _____ soup.

2 What did Selena buy?

Vocabulary | Look at the picture. Write what Selena bought at the grocery store.

1. _a jar of olives_
2. _____
3. _____
4. _____
5. _____
6. _____
7. _____
8. _____

3 A lot or a little?

Grammar | Carl is doing his weekly grocery shopping. Circle the best quantifier to complete each of his thoughts.

Hmm . . . we only have **a few** / **a little** cheese left in the refrigerator. I guess I'll get some more. And there's **not many** / **not much** butter left, either, so I'll get some of that, too. I don't think that there are **many** / **much** oranges left in the fruit bowl, and I know my roommate likes bananas, so I'll get both. He's such a picky eater. He eats **very few** / **very little** vegetables, but I should get **a few** / **a little** peppers, at least. Um . . . the ice-cream section . . . I really want to eat **fewer** / **less** ice cream, but maybe I can buy a light, fat-free kind with **fewer** / **less** calories in it. Well, I think that's all I need. . . .

4 About you

Grammar and vocabulary | Complete each sentence with true information. Use a quantifier from the box and a food word. The quantifiers may be used more than once.

a few	fewer	very few
a little	less	very little

1. There are _very few apples_ in my refrigerator.
2. I try to eat _____ every day.
3. I had _____ yesterday.
4. I'm eating _____ these days.
5. There's _____ in my cupboard.
6. I eat _____ than I used to.

1 Prepared foods

Vocabulary | There are ten ways to serve foods in the puzzle. Find the other nine.
Look in these directions (→↓).

B	A	K	E	D	X	L	Y	Q	B
A	B	L	M	A	R	R	T	E	G
R	O	A	S	T	P	A	I	P	R
B	I	C	M	R	Z	W	Y	I	I
E	L	S	M	O	K	E	D	C	L
C	E	D	C	J	E	L	M	K	L
U	D	F	R	I	E	D	P	L	E
E	Z	T	S	T	E	A	M	E	D
D	M	U	X	P	Y	R	I	D	P

2 Smoked bread?

Vocabulary | Cross out the food that is the least likely to go with the preparation.
Then replace it with an appropriate food.

1. smoked ⎰ cheese
    ⎱ turkey
    ⎰ ~~bread~~ *fish*

2. raw ⎰ fish
    ⎱ ice cream
    ⎰ vegetables

3. boiled ⎰ grapes
    ⎱ eggs
    ⎰ potatoes

4. steamed ⎰ rice
    ⎱ milk
    ⎰ pizza

5. fried ⎰ noodles
    ⎱ yogurt
    ⎰ chicken

6. barbecued ⎰ noodles
    ⎱ beef
    ⎰ lamb

7. pickled ⎰ cabbage
    ⎱ cucumbers
    ⎰ cheese

3 Too much rice

Grammar | **What's the problem? Complete the sentences with *too*, *too much*, *too many*, or *enough*.**

1. Martha got _too much_ rice and not ___enough___ meat.

2. Sheila ate _____ cupcakes!
   She often eats _____ dessert.

3. This coffee costs _____ !
   It's _____ expensive.

4. Taro drank the lemonade
   _____ fast.

5. The soup's not hot _____ .
   And there's _____ salt in it.

6. Alice didn't take the turkey out early
   _____ . Now she won't have
   _____ food for dinner.

4 About you

Grammar and vocabulary | **Complete the questions with *too*, *too much*, *too many*, or *enough*.
Then write true answers.**

1. Do you eat a lot of snacks? Do you eat _too many_ ? _I eat three snacks a day._

2. Do you eat _____ vegetables every day? _____

3. Do you ever feel _____ full after eating a meal? _____

4. Do you exercise _____ – at least twice a week? _____

5. Do you eat _____ for lunch so you don't need a snack later? _____

6. Do you ever eat meals _____ quickly and feel sick? _____

7. Do you drink _____ water – at least two liters every day? _____

8. Do you think you eat _____ fried foods? _____

1 Either way is fine.

Complete the conversation with the expressions in the box.

either one is fine	whatever you're having
either way is fine	✓ whichever is easier for you

Brent   I'm going to cook dinner tonight,
so what would you like? Chicken or steak?

Imani   Well, you're the cook,
so _whichever is easier for you_ .

Brent   No, I want you to choose. I got to decide last night's dinner menu.

Imani   Well, you know, I really like both,
so _____ .

Brent   OK. I'll cook the chicken. How do you want it tonight? Fried or grilled?

Imani   Oh, _____ . I'm sure whatever you cook will be delicious.

Brent   OK, I'll grill it. Now, what do you want to drink?

Imani   Oh, _____ . You know me, anything is fine.

Brent   Well, you're certainly easy to please!

Imani   I try.

2 Whatever you want.

Imagine you are at a friend's house. Respond to each question appropriately to let your friend decide.

Friend   Do you want to eat out or get takeout later tonight?

You   _Oh, I don't care. Whatever you prefer._

Friend   OK, let's go out. Do you prefer Mexican or Indian food?

You   _____

Friend   Well, I know this great Mexican restaurant. I'll make reservations. 7:00 or 8:00?

You   _____

Friend   Oh, let's make it 7:30. Now, should we drive or take the subway?

You   _____

Friend   Well, driving is easier, so should we take your car or mine?

You   _____

Friend   All right. I'll drive. Now, would you like something to drink? Tea? Coffee?

You   _____

3 I'm OK for now.

Conversation strategies **Use polite refusal expressions to complete the conversation.**

Peggy   Would you like some more iced tea?

Nora   _No, thanks. Maybe later._   I've got enough here.

Peggy   Gosh, there were a lot of fries here. I still have some left. Would you like a few?

Nora   _____ I'm trying to cut down on things like fries. You didn't have much salad. Take some of my carrots.

Peggy   _____ You know, they have the best chocolate cake here. You should try some.

Nora   _____ I'm trying to eat less sugar, too.

Peggy   Oh. Well, are you going to have coffee?

Nora   _____

4 Let's have some . . .

Conversation strategies **Respond to each question by politely refusing or letting the other person decide.**

1. Let's have some ice cream. Would you like vanilla or strawberry?

   Either one is fine. Whatever you're having.

2. I'm getting hungry. Do you want something to eat?

   _____

3. There's cake and cookies for dessert. Which would you like?

   _____

4. I'm going to bake a pie. Do you prefer apple or peach?

   _____

5. I'm taking you to lunch today! Would you like Italian or Thai?

   _____

1 Food alternatives

Reading | **A** Read the article. Circle the helpful foods and products that are mentioned.

DOUBLE DUTY

Did you know that you have a personal beauty spa right in your refrigerator? And did you know that for easy fix-it projects around your home, you simply need to look at your grocery list for help? Here are some ways to make your groceries do double duty.

Hair and face care

BRIGHTER EYES Were you up all night studying for a test, and now it's morning, and your eyes are tired and puffy? Take a few slices of a cold cucumber, and place them over your eyes. Leave them on for about 5 to 10 minutes. Good-bye puffiness, good morning bright eyes!

CLEARER SKIN Uh-oh. You've got a date this weekend, and you just woke up with a pimple! Take a little toothpaste – not too much – and put it on the pimple. Leave it on for at least 5 minutes. Repeat daily if necessary. By Saturday night, your date won't notice a thing!

LIGHTER HAIR Do you want some summer highlights and can't afford a hair salon? The next time you're going out in the sun, squeeze some fresh lemon juice into a bowl, and comb it through your hair.

Fix-it projects

WATER STAINS Did you leave a cold glass of water on a wooden table overnight, and now there's a ring on it? You can't make it disappear, but you can lighten it considerably – with

toothpaste. Mix equal parts toothpaste and baking soda, and then rub the mixture into the wood with a damp cloth. Wipe it off with a dry cloth.

CLOGGED DRAIN Is your shower drain clogged, and now the water's taking a long time to go down? Mix equal parts salt, baking soda, and cream of tartar, and then pour it down the drain. Follow with boiling water. Leave it overnight.

Pest remedy

INSECT BITES One thing about summer you can't control is the bugs. But you can stop them from biting you. White vinegar will deter some pests. Pour some vinegar onto a cloth, and wipe over your skin. The smell goes away after the vinegar has dried, but the bugs won't like the taste of the vinegar. Reapply often.

B Read the article again. Then match the two parts of each sentence.

1. For puffy eyes, _d_
2. To get rid of pimples, ____
3. To lighten your hair, ____
4. To treat a water stain on wood, ____
5. To unclog a drain, ____
6. To deter biting pests, ____

a. wipe vinegar on your skin.
b. put baking soda, cream of tartar, and salt in it.
c. rub toothpaste and baking soda on it.
d. place cucumber slices on them.
e. comb lemon juice through it.
f. put a little toothpaste on them.

2 Ethnic eateries

Writing **A** Read the article about healthy eating habits in Okinawa. Add *for example*, *like*, or *such as* to introduce examples. Often more than one is correct.

Food as the Secret to Good Health

If you want to live to be 100 years old, you may want to try the Okinawan diet. People on Okinawa live a very long time. Although Okinawa is part of Japan, the diet is a little different. _____ , people eat a lot of green vegetables, _____ broccoli and green beans. In fact, about three quarters of their diet is vegetables, fruit, and whole grains. Only about 3% comes from meat, poultry, and eggs. They also eat more soybean products, _____ tofu. They don't eat many foods that have a lot of fat, _____ , cheese.

B Write an article about healthy foods that people eat in your country. Give examples using *for example*, *like*, and *such as*.

_____

_____

_____

_____

_____

_____

Unit 5 Progress chart

What can you do? Mark the boxes. ✔ = I can . . . ? = I need to review how to . . .	To review, go back to these pages in the Student's Book.
Grammar ☐ use quantifiers like *a little*, *a few*, *very little*, *very few*, etc.	44 and 45
☐ use *too*, *too much*, *too many*, and *enough*.	47
Vocabulary ☐ talk about food using expressions like *a jar of*, *a can of*, *a box of*, etc.	43 and 44
☐ name at least 8 different ways of serving food.	46
Conversation strategies ☐ respond to questions by letting another person decide.	48
☐ use expressions like *No, thanks. I'm fine* to refuse an offer politely.	49
Writing ☐ use *for example*, *like*, and *such as* to introduce examples.	51

Managing life

UNIT 6

Lesson A / Making plans

1 What are you doing after work?

Grammar | Circle the best verb forms to complete the conversations.

1. **Ahmed** Hey, Finn. What **do you do** / **are you doing** after work tonight?

   Finn I have no plans. **I just go** / **I'm just going home**. Why? What are you up to?

   Ahmed Well, **I go** / **I'm going** to the gym around 5:00, but after that, I have no plans.

   Finn OK. Well, maybe **I'm stopping by** / **I'll stop by** later.

   Ahmed Sure. **I make** / **I'll make** dinner.

   Finn Oh, no. I just remembered. **I have** / **I'm having** a doctor's appointment at 6:00.

   Ahmed That's OK. **I'm waiting** / **I'll wait** for you to eat. Just come right over when you're done.

   Finn All right. **I'm going to be** / **I'll be** there by 7:30.

   Ahmed Don't be late!

2. **Leah** Hi, Mom. I was just calling to let you know that **I take** / **I'm going to take** a 5:30 train this Friday.

   Mom Great, honey. **I'm meeting** / **I'll meet** you at the station.

   Leah No, that's OK. **I won't need** / **I'm not needing** you to pick me up. **I get** / **I'll get** a taxi.

   Mom OK. **Do you bring** / **Are you bringing** your friend?

   Leah Yeah. Janice **will come** / **is coming** with me.

   Mom Oh, how nice. I can't wait to meet her!

   Leah I'm sure **you're going to like** / **you like** her. See you Friday!

2 Let me check my schedule.

Grammar | Look at Millie's weekly planner, and complete the conversation. Use the verbs in parentheses and the information from the planner.

Monday	**Thursday**
~~art exhibit with Jenna~~	6:30 guitar lesson, as usual
Tuesday	**Friday**
6:30 guitar lesson	plans with Heidi?
Wednesday	**Saturday** dinner with Greg
5:45 eye doctor appointment	**Sunday** 7:00 flight

Raquel   Let's have dinner together this week.

Millie   Sounds good. I'd love to catch up with you.

Raquel   How about Saturday?

Millie   Hmm . . . I can't Saturday. I _'m meeting / 'm going to meet Greg for dinner_ (meet).

Raquel   Well, then, what about Thursday?

Millie   That won't work, either. I _____ (have).

Raquel   Oh, yeah, I forgot. Well, I'm free next Sunday.

Millie   Sunday I'm leaving for Dallas. My flight _____ (leave).

Raquel   And Friday?

Millie   I may have plans with Heidi.

Raquel   Oh? What are you guys doing?

Millie   I don't know. I _____ (call) on Friday to see what's up.

Raquel   OK. Well, then why don't *you* pick a day?

Millie   Let's see . . . Oh, Wednesday, I _____ (have). Actually, you know what? Jenna canceled our plans to see an art exhibit tonight. Do you want to go?

Raquel   Sure. I _____ (go) with you!

3 About you

Grammar | Answer the questions with true information.

1. What are you going to do tonight?

    _____

2. Are you doing anything special this weekend?

    _____

3. Do you have any appointments this month? If yes, who with?

    _____

4. Who are you having dinner with tomorrow night?

    _____

5. What do you think you'll do when you finish this exercise?

    _____

1 Make up your mind.

Vocabulary | **A** Complete the *make* and *do* expressions. Use the definitions to help you.

1. make a __*living*__ = work to earn money
2. make a good _____ = make someone think of you positively
3. make a _____ = make a positive change
4. do your _____ = try your hardest
5. make up your _____ = decide
6. make _____ of = make jokes about and laugh at
7. make _____ = make certain
8. make a _____ = get something wrong
9. do the _____ = figure out the numbers
10. make _____ = seem logical

B Complete the conversations with the *make* and *do* expressions from part A.

1. A Which computer are you going to get?
   Did you __*make up your mind*__?

   B No. I can't decide. I like this one, but it's expensive.

   A Well, buy the best you can afford.
   It doesn't _____ to buy a cheap one.

   B Yeah, you're right. I need to _____
   and look at all the numbers before I decide.

2. A Are you all prepared for your interview? You look
   great. I'm sure you'll _____ .

   B Thanks. I really want this job with the children's
   charity. I've always wanted to _____
   in people's lives. I know it's not well paid, but it's how
   I want to _____ .

   A Well, good luck. You'd better leave now
   to _____ you get there on time.

3. A I have to give a presentation to the class today.
   I'm so afraid I'll _____ and say
   something wrong.

   B Well, just _____ , and I'm sure
   everything will be fine.

   A I know. I'm just scared that the other students
   will _____ me.

2 Let's ask Daphne.

Grammar | **Circle the best expression to complete each sentence.**

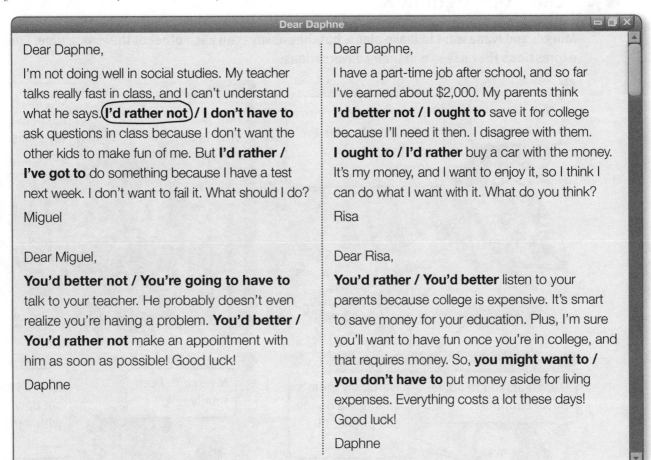

Dear Daphne   ▭ ▢ ✕

Dear Daphne,

I'm not doing well in social studies. My teacher
talks really fast in class, and I can't understand
what he says. (**I'd rather not**) / **I don't have to**
ask questions in class because I don't want the
other kids to make fun of me. But **I'd rather /
I've got to** do something because I have a test
next week. I don't want to fail it. What should I do?

Miguel

Dear Daphne,

I have a part-time job after school, and so far
I've earned about $2,000. My parents think
I'd better not / I ought to save it for college
because I'll need it then. I disagree with them.
I ought to / I'd rather buy a car with the money.
It's my money, and I want to enjoy it, so I think I
can do what I want with it. What do you think?

Risa

Dear Miguel,

You'd better not / You're going to have to
talk to your teacher. He probably doesn't even
realize you're having a problem. **You'd better /
You'd rather not** make an appointment with
him as soon as possible! Good luck!

Daphne

Dear Risa,

You'd rather / You'd better listen to your
parents because college is expensive. It's smart
to save money for your education. Plus, I'm sure
you'll want to have fun once you're in college, and
that requires money. So, **you might want to /
you don't have to** put money aside for living
expenses. Everything costs a lot these days!
Good luck!

Daphne

3 About you

Grammar | **Write true sentences about these topics.**

1. something you've got to do this week
   I've got to make up my mind about a summer job.
   _____

2. something you'd better do before next week
   _____

3. two things you don't have to do this week
   _____

4. something you feel you ought to do this year
   _____

5. something you'd rather do now instead of homework
   _____

6. three things you're going to have to do tomorrow
   _____

1 I can't talk right now.

Conversation
strategies
Ming-li and Ivana want to make plans, but they always call each other at the wrong time. Complete the expressions they use to end their conversations.

1

Hey, Ming-li. It's Ivana.

Hi, Ivana. Listen, I can't talk. I have to walk the dog. I've got _to go_ .

2

Hey, Ivana. I'm back. What's up?

Oh, no. Now I can't talk. I'm going to my yoga class. I've got to get _____ .

3

Oh, great, you're home. Have a minute?

Ivana, my mom's calling me on my cell phone. I'll _____ .

4

Me again. I can finally talk.

Hey. Listen, I just sat down to dinner with a friend. I'd _____ .

5

Hey. I just got back from dinner.

Ivana, it's midnight! Can I _____ tomorrow morning?

6

So, I got tickets to Friday's concert. Do you want to go?

Sure! Listen, call me Friday. I'm going _____ . I have a meeting.

2 Talk to you later!

Conversation strategies **Circle the best response. Then write the shorter form.**

1. A Oh, hi. Can I call you back later?
    B _Sure. Talk to you later._
      a. Sure. I'd better go.
      b. Sure. I'll talk to you later. ⟨circled⟩

2. A I'm really sorry. I've got to go out in two minutes.
    B _____
      a. No problem. I've got to go, too. Bye.
      b. No problem. I'm not busy.

3. A Let's talk tomorrow.
    B _____
      a. OK. Now's a good time.
      b. OK. I'll catch you later.

4. A Well, anyway, I'd better go.
    B _____
      a. OK. I'll see you later.
      b. OK. I can't talk right now.

5. A I'm so glad you called. It was fun to catch up.
    B _____
      a. Yeah, I'll call you later.
      b. Yeah, it was nice talking to you, too!

6. A I'd better go. I'm late.
    B _____
      a. That's OK. I'm free now.
      b. That's OK. I'd better go, too.

3 The end?

Conversation strategies **Imagine you're trying to leave your house to go to your English class, but four friends call you. Try to end each conversation. Then use a "friendly" good-bye.**

1. Liliana Hi, it's me. Listen, I have a problem. Do you have some time to talk?
    You _Not really. I've got to go to English class. Can I call you back?_
    Liliana OK.
    You _Talk to you later._

2. Hans Hi, it's Hans. Are you busy right now? I need to ask you a question.
    You _____
    Hans No problem.
    You _____

3. Doug Hey! Guess what? I have some exciting news for you!
    You _____
    Doug Fine. Call me when you get home later.
    You _____

4. Louisa Hi! It's Louisa. I didn't understand the homework. Did you?
    You _____
    Louisa All right. Well, maybe we can meet in the library tomorrow.
    You _____

1 Getting organized

Reading | **A** Read the article. Then add the correct heading to each section.

Save money   Save space   Save time

$ $ $ $ $ $ $ $ $ $ Tips that $ave $ $ $ $ $ $ $ $ $ $

Whether your schedule is crazy, your apartment is cluttered, or your budget is mismanaged, here are some tips to get more organized.

[   ]

Do you find it difficult to find really good birthday presents because you wait until the last minute? And then do you spend hours in the stores because you can't find anything you like?

Whenever you're shopping and you see a gift at a great price, buy it and put it in your closet. When a special occasion comes up and you need a gift for someone, you'll have a selection of things to choose from. You won't have to make a special trip for last-minute shopping.

Do you ever pay bills late because you lose them in all the papers and clutter in your home? Well, if you need a system for paying your bills on time, the trick is to pay them online. You can arrange to pay your bills directly from your bank account. Once you have set up online bill pay, you can either set up a reminder for yourself to pay on a certain date, or you can have your bills paid automatically.

[   ]

Magazines can take over your home before you know it. Most magazines are also available online. Save space by reading the articles online.

Or, if you like to read a print magazine and want to save an article, go online and download the article to your computer. Then read it again whenever you want.

Buy brightly colored baskets or boxes for your shelves to store smaller items neatly. Label them with their contents. Your shelves will look neater, and you'll have more space for your larger items. Hang single shelves above doorways to store things you rarely use. Place low shelves in your closet to take advantage of unused space.

[   ]

Save for a rainy day, little by little. It's easy to make progress if you give yourself a weekly allowance. Try to spend less than your allowance each week. Put the remaining money in an envelope. At the end of each month, put the money in your bank account.

It's the little habits that count. Have you added up the cost of those cappuccinos you buy every morning? If you spend $3.50 on coffee five days a week, that adds up to $910 a year! By doing without fancy drinks and making your coffee at home, you can save a bundle. You might want to try packing a lunch instead of eating at the local café, too – this habit can also save you hundreds a year.

B Find these words and expressions in the article. Match them with the definitions.

1. clutter __e__
2. the trick _____
3. take advantage of _____
4. a rainy day _____
5. count _____
6. doing without _____
7. a bundle _____

a. make use of
b. a time when you need money
c. not having
d. a lot of money
e. mess
f. make a difference
g. best thing to do

C Read the article again. Then write *T* (true), *F* (false), or *D* (doesn't say).

1. _T_ Buy gifts cheaply when you see them; you can decide who they're for later.

2. ____ You can save money if you pay your bills late.

3. ____ Downloading articles to your computer is a good way to save time.

4. ____ You can save space on your shelves if you put lots of small things into boxes.

5. ____ It's better to keep your money in an envelope than a bank.

6. ____ You should make more food at home.

2 Making room

Writing **A** Read the article. Add *as long as*, *provided that*, and *unless* to link ideas. Sometimes more than one answer is possible.

> Your closet is overflowing, and you need to make room for new clothes. How do you decide what to do with all your old clothes? First, get a box and put in everything you hardly ever wear, _____ they aren't clothes for special occasions.
>
> Give them all to a charity store _____ you have some valuable clothes you can sell. Next, use the "two-season rule." Separate your remaining clothes by season. If it's winter, put your winter clothes back in the closet. Buy some under-the-bed boxes for your off-season clothes. If it's summer, store all your sweaters under your bed, _____ the space under your bed isn't already cluttered!

B Write a short article giving advice about how to reduce clutter, save money, or save time. Try to use *as long as*, *provided that*, and *unless* to link ideas.

Unit 6 Progress chart

What can you do? Mark the boxes. ☑ = I can . . . ? = I need to review how to . . .	To review, go back to these pages in the Student's Book.
Grammar ▪ talk about the future using *will*, *going to*, the present continuous, and the simple present.	54 and 55
▪ use *ought to*, *have got to*, *would rather*, *had better*, etc.	56 and 57
Vocabulary ▪ use at least 12 expressions with *do* or *make*.	56
Conversation strategies ▪ use at least 5 different expressions to end a phone conversation.	58
▪ say good-bye in an informal, friendly way.	59
Writing ▪ use *as long as*, *provided that*, and *unless* to link ideas.	61

Illustration credits

Harry Briggs: 22, 42, 80　　**Cambridge University Press:** 21, 50　　**Steve Cancel:** 93　　**Chuck Gonzales:** 13, 37, 58, 82, 83
Frank Montagna: 2, 26, 27, 44, 67, 86, 87　　**Marilena Perilli:** 6, 7, 20, 28, 46, 62, 63, 74　　**Greg White:** 14, 35, 78, 91
Terry Wong: 5, 38, 39, 54, 68, 69, 94, 95

Photo credits

3 ©Andresr/Shutterstock　**4** ©Erin Patrice O'Brien/Getty　**8** *(top to bottom)* ©Michael Tran/FilmMagic/Getty Images; ©Eros International/courtesy Everett Collection　**9** ©Monirul Alam/ZUMAPRESS.com/Alamy　**10** *(left to right)* ©Alexandra Lande/Shutterstock; ©GoodSportHD.com/Alamy　**11** ©Eyecandy Images/Alamy　**12** *(top to bottom)* ©Yadid Levy/age fotostock/SuperStock; ©Andrew Bain/Getty Images; ©Manfred Grebler/Getty Images; ©Universal Images Group/SuperStock　**15** *(left to right)* ©Philip Lee Harvey/Getty Images; ©Punchstock　**16** *(top to bottom)* ©Oktay Ortakcioglu/Getty Images; ©leungchopan/Shutterstock　**18** *(top row, left to right)* ©Francesco Dazzi/Shutterstock; ©Medioimages/Photodisc/Thinkstock; ©Maurilio Cheli/Associated Press; ©Max Nash/Associated Press *(bottom row, left to right)* ©Jerritt Clark/WireImage/Getty Images; ©Randy Faris/Corbis; ©Alik Keplicz/Associated Press; ©Mike Segar/Reuters/Newscom　**19** ©Andrzej Gorzkowski Photography/Alamy　**20** *(clockwise from top left)* ©Punchstock; ©Thinkstock; ©Digital Vision/Thinkstock; ©Thinkstock; ©AAMIR QURESHI/AFP/Getty Images; ©Galen Rowell/Corbis　**23** ©Thinkstock　**24** ©Photo Courtesy of NOAA *(background)* ©Serg Zastavkin/Shutterstock *(icicles)* ©April Cat/Shutterstock　**25** ©Thinkstock　**29** ©imagebroker.net/SuperStock　**32** ©Frank Herholdt/Getty Images　**34** ©George Kerrigan　**35** ©George Kerrigan　**36** *(top to bottom)* ©ifong/Shutterstock; ©Stockvision/Shutterstock　**40** ©Thinkstock　**41** *(top to bottom)* ©Robyn Mackenzie/Shutterstock; ©Lucky Business/Shutterstock　**50** *(top to bottom)* ©Thinkstock; ©Punchstock; ©Dennis MacDonald/Age Fotostock; ©Sherrianne Talon/istockphoto; ©Jurgen Reisch/Getty Images　**53** ©Rich Legg/Getty Images　**55** *(all photos)* ©Thinkstock　**59** ©x7vector/Shutterstock　**61** ©Andrew D. Bernstein/NBAE via Getty Images　**62** ©John Giustina/Getty Images　**66** ©MediaBakery　**70** ©PBS/Courtesy: Everett Collection　**75** ©Clark Brennan/Alamy　**77** ©Jupiterimages/Thinkstock　**80** *(top)* ©DircinhaSW/Getty Images *(bottom, left to right)* ©JGI/Getty Images/RF; ©Cultura Limited/SuperStock　**81** ©David Wolff-Patrick/WireImage/Getty Images　**84** *(clockwise from top left)* ©Punchstock; ©Nick Chaldakov/Alamy; ©Thinkstock; ©Digital Vision/Thinkstock　**90** *(top to bottom)* ©Mike Finn-Kelcey/Newscom; ©RubberBall/SuperStock; ©Thinkstock　**92** *(clockwise from top left)* ©Sandra Mu/Getty Images; ©David Cole/Alamy; ©Thinkstock; ©Thinkstock; ©Thinkstock; ©Eric Nguyen/Jim Reed Photography/Corbis

Text credits

While every effort has been made, it has not always been possible to identify the sources of all the materials used, or to trace all copyright holders. If any omissions are brought to our notice, we will be happy to include the appropriate acknowledgements on reprinting.

The top 500 spoken words

This is a list of the top 500 words in spoken North American English. It is based on a sample of four and a half million words of conversation from the Cambridge International Corpus. The most frequent word, *I*, is at the top of the list.

1. I	40. really	79. see
2. and	41. with	80. how
3. the	42. he	81. they're
4. you	43. one	82. kind
5. uh	44. are	83. here
6. to	45. this	84. from
7. a	46. there	85. did
8. that	47. I'm	86. something
9. it	48. all	87. too
10. of	49. if	88. more
11. yeah	50. no	89. very
12. know	51. get	90. want
13. in	52. about	91. little
14. like	53. at	92. been
15. they	54. out	93. things
16. have	55. had	94. an
17. so	56. then	95. you're
18. was	57. because	96. said
19. but	58. go	97. there's
20. is	59. up	98. I've
21. it's	60. she	99. much
22. we	61. when	100. where
23. huh	62. them	101. two
24. just	63. can	102. thing
25. oh	64. would	103. her
26. do	65. as	104. didn't
27. don't	66. me	105. other
28. that's	67. mean	106. say
29. well	68. some	107. back
30. for	69. good	108. could
31. what	70. got	109. their
32. on	71. OK	110. our
33. think	72. people	111. guess
34. right	73. now	112. yes
35. not	74. going	113. way
36. um	75. were	114. has
37. or	76. lot	115. down
38. my	77. your	116. we're
39. be	78. time	117. any

The top 500 spoken words

118. he's	161. five	204. sort
119. work	162. always	205. great
120. take	163. school	206. bad
121. even	164. look	207. we've
122. those	165. still	208. another
123. over	166. around	209. car
124. probably	167. anything	210. true
125. him	168. kids	211. whole
126. who	169. first	212. whatever
127. put	170. does	213. twenty
128. years	171. need	214. after
129. sure	172. us	215. ever
130. can't	173. should	216. find
131. pretty	174. talking	217. care
132. gonna	175. last	218. better
133. stuff	176. thought	219. hard
134. come	177. doesn't	220. haven't
135. these	178. different	221. trying
136. by	179. money	222. give
137. into	180. long	223. I'd
138. went	181. used	224. problem
139. make	182. getting	225. else
140. than	183. same	226. remember
141. year	184. four	227. might
142. three	185. every	228. again
143. which	186. new	229. pay
144. home	187. everything	230. try
145. will	188. many	231. place
146. nice	189. before	232. part
147. never	190. though	233. let
148. only	191. most	234. keep
149. his	192. tell	235. children
150. doing	193. being	236. anyway
151. cause	194. bit	237. came
152. off	195. house	238. six
153. I'll	196. also	239. family
154. maybe	197. use	240. wasn't
155. real	198. through	241. talk
156. why	199. feel	242. made
157. big	200. course	243. hundred
158. actually	201. what's	244. night
159. she's	202. old	245. call
160. day	203. done	246. saying

The top 500 spoken words

247. dollars	290. started	333. believe
248. live	291. job	334. thinking
249. away	292. says	335. funny
250. either	293. play	336. state
251. read	294. usually	337. until
252. having	295. wow	338. husband
253. far	296. exactly	339. idea
254. watch	297. took	340. name
255. week	298. few	341. seven
256. mhm	299. child	342. together
257. quite	300. thirty	343. each
258. enough	301. buy	344. hear
259. next	302. person	345. help
260. couple	303. working	346. nothing
261. own	304. half	347. parents
262. wouldn't	305. looking	348. room
263. ten	306. someone	349. today
264. interesting	307. coming	350. makes
265. am	308. eight	351. stay
266. sometimes	309. love	352. mom
267. bye	310. everybody	353. sounds
268. seems	311. able	354. change
269. heard	312. we'll	355. understand
270. goes	313. life	356. such
271. called	314. may	357. gone
272. point	315. both	358. system
273. ago	316. type	359. comes
274. while	317. end	360. thank
275. fact	318. least	361. show
276. once	319. told	362. thousand
277. seen	320. saw	363. left
278. wanted	321. college	364. friends
279. isn't	322. ones	365. class
280. start	323. almost	366. already
281. high	324. since	367. eat
282. somebody	325. days	368. small
283. let's	326. couldn't	369. boy
284. times	327. gets	370. paper
285. guy	328. guys	371. world
286. area	329. god	372. best
287. fun	330. country	373. water
288. they've	331. wait	374. myself
289. you've	332. yet	375. run

The top 500 spoken words

376. they'll	418. company	460. sorry
377. won't	419. friend	461. living
378. movie	420. set	462. drive
379. cool	421. minutes	463. outside
380. news	422. morning	464. bring
381. number	423. between	465. easy
382. man	424. music	466. stop
383. basically	425. close	467. percent
384. nine	426. leave	468. hand
385. enjoy	427. wife	469. gosh
386. bought	428. knew	470. top
387. whether	429. pick	471. cut
388. especially	430. important	472. computer
389. taking	431. ask	473. tried
390. sit	432. hour	474. gotten
391. book	433. deal	475. mind
392. fifty	434. mine	476. business
393. months	435. reason	477. anybody
394. women	436. credit	478. takes
395. month	437. dog	479. aren't
396. found	438. group	480. question
397. side	439. turn	481. rather
398. food	440. making	482. twelve
399. looks	441. American	483. phone
400. summer	442. weeks	484. program
401. hmm	443. certain	485. without
402. fine	444. less	486. moved
403. hey	445. must	487. gave
404. student	446. dad	488. yep
405. agree	447. during	489. case
406. mother	448. lived	490. looked
407. problems	449. forty	491. certainly
408. city	450. air	492. talked
409. second	451. government	493. beautiful
410. definitely	452. eighty	494. card
411. spend	453. wonderful	495. walk
412. happened	454. seem	496. married
413. hours	455. wrong	497. anymore
414. war	456. young	498. you'll
415. matter	457. places	499. middle
416. supposed	458. girl	500. tax
417. worked	459. happen	